A Little Spot of Poetry

Lisa Ride

Print information available on the last page

Rev. date: 10/14/2016

To order additional copies of this book, contact:
Xlibris
1-800-455-039
www.xlibris.com.au
Orders@Xlibris.com.au

A Little Spot of Poetry
PO Box 267
Kiewa Street Post Office
Albury NSW 2640
AUSTRALIA

Dedicated to Josie Lester with love

To those who encouraged along the way: Giles Pickford, Susan Palmer, Dr. Andrew Kingsford, Ian and Brenda Whittingslow, Sandy Beattie, Amanda Reis, Jan Lewis, Carol Reffold, Glenys Stratfold, Ruth Rawson, Barbara Craven-Griffiths, Sinead Murphy, Wendy and Sandy Tymczuk, Tracy Caines and Louise McManus.

And remembering Dottie the Dalmatian who left pawprints on my heart.

Photo by Graham Tidy/1992/Fairfax Syndication

Lisa Ride was born and raised in Canberra ACT, attending Garran Primary School and Canberra Girls Grammar (1974-1979) where her love of writing was fostered. Studying at (the now) University of Canberra in 1980, she took up the offer of a travelling recruiting company to join the fledgling Australian Federal Police (AFP) as an Undergraduate. During the late eighties and nineties Lisa was well known in Canberra as the police public relations spokesperson for the uniformed component of the AFP. She is pictured in 1992 with one of her Luckywood Dalmatian puppies.

Lisa went on to work as the Media Liaison Manager for the Australian National University (ANU); as a NSW Corrections Court Escort & Security Officer; a Case Manager for Community Offender Services and as a Civil Marriage Celebrant (2004-2014) Lisa also proudly served in the Australian Army Reserve (1981-2016). Affected by Parkinson's she maintains positivity by singing as an Alto in the Royal School of Church Music system and continues to support Defence personnel by making Aussie Hero Quilts for deployed soldiers. In addition she's a mother of five and grandmother of one.

A Little Spot of Poetry is a collection of 22 poems written by Lisa who describes herself as "the poet with Parkinson's writing in the style of Pam Ayres meets A. B. Paterson". Along the way Dottie the Dalmatian shares in her adventures.

Lisa's first public poetry recital was at the ANU Poets' Lunch in 1995 where her poem ***Ode to Berocca*** was chosen for publication. Her poem ***The Fabric Stash*** is known to quilt groups all over the world. Lisa's first delivery of performance poetry was at Beechworth WRAP in 2014. Since that time she has won 'New Novice Writer' at the Australian National Bush Poetry Championships with ***Driving to Corryong*** in 2015; was a state finalist (Victoria) in the 2015 Australian Poetry Slam after a crowd pleasing performance of ***My Mother Said*** at Wangaratta and is a state finalist for NSW (Albury) in the 2016 Australian Poetry Slam with ***Domestic Bliss***. She was also a winner at the 2016 Victorian Performance Bush Poetry competition (Lawrie Sheridan Award). Her most popular poem ***Remember the Australian Soldier*** *"is a moving tribute to those who serve"* (The Border Mail).

Contents

Ode to Berocca

In 1995 I went to work for the ANU as their Media Liaison Manager after my time as a general duties (uniformed) police officer in Canberra with the AFP. This poem was submitted after encouragement from Mr. Giles Pickford of ANU's Public Affairs Division.

My cheeky poem was chosen for printing in the **ANU Poets' Lunch** booklet of 1995 among many accomplished poets' work and I had to read it on ABC Radio. I have left the poem as I wrote it but I must confess I would substitute a *Boags* for the VB these days!

Oh Berocca!
Thy humble servant
I beseech thee, fix mine head
The sun is high
I have arisen.....not
I cannot stumble from my bed

The distant banging, an ungodly noise
I wonder from where it comes?
I cannot focus
On life before me
The noise!
It comes from within!

Bubbling, purple liquid
Flowing, feeding, nourishing
Save me from my evil undoing
Unburden my troubled soul
My panacea to all consumption
Of beer, golden and gold

Ah, beer!
God's own creation
Bubbles gently rising
Stark, white frothy head
The smell of hops.......

Stuff the Berocca
I'll have a VB instead!

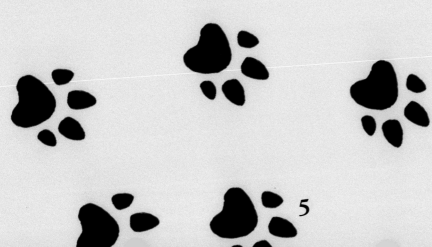

My Mother Said

My mother Josie Lester was born in Gravesend, Kent in 1931. In 1956 she left England to work as a stenographer at the British High Commission in Canberra, Australia. Don't dare refer to her as a *ten-pound pom* or she'll go off! My mother had a fine voice and played *The Lovers* in Canberra Repertory's production of **The Sentimental Bloke.** Here she met my father Edwin Ride and in 1957 they were married from Lawley House which was later to become the AFP College where I trained as a police officer.

For a while my father left full-time employment with Foreign Affairs & Trade to play *The Bloke* in Albert Arlen's musical stage production of the same name. Josie was to remain in Canberra as she had fallen pregnant and sadly before me, had two stillborn sons. The next time I saw my father I was 19—but that's another story.

She refused to be called Mum and we all called her Moosie. Moosie brought some quirky British ideas to Australia. I was the only child at Garran Primary who went to school with cream cheese and sultana sandwiches. Rules such as: you should always dress to fly, and I still do. My mother had dozens of sayings (as most mothers do) and I wanted to pen a poem about them. The first time I recited *My Mother Said* to her I was apprehensive about her reaction but she laughed and said: "That's fabulous, and *my* mother would have loved it too!"

Reciting this poem at the **Australian National Bush Poetry Championships** in 2015, I won *Best Intermediate Performance*. It is still one of my personal favourites.

My mother gave another sigh
Her bosom heaved in sad reply
And as she leaned upon the sink
She said "What will the neighbours think?"
There are many sayings mother taught us
And some I've passed on to my daughters
But some are old and seem to be
Fading to obscurity

You see there's no such thing as in-between
As kids Twitter, twerk, and blog their screen
Children used to read upon my lap
But now all they need is a smart app
And I do hate it when they sit and stare
At my Motorola Flare.[1]
For even grannies seem to have it made
With every iPhone they upgrade

At my twenty first I got a key
But now all open electronically
And things have changed at such a rate
That children cannot demonstrate
Such things as chasey, hide and seek
Or run through willows by the creek

When I was four I used to skip
Milk bottle in hand, my daily trip
Through underpass just near our shop
Past the homeless man—and there I'd stop!
"Is there anything at all you need today?"
And then I'd run and skip and play

_____

1 A chunky mobile phone from 1995.

I'm sure that if I did that now
I'd not return (I know not how)
And all that there'd be left of me
Would be *Crimestoppers* on TV
My lifeless body with red strings and lines
On a detective's whiteboard intertwined
To show that children should never stray
From parents' safety, far away

And God forbid, if I should slip
With glass in hand, well, then I'd sit
At A&E for thirty hours
Just to feel life's fateful powers
In years gone by all I would see
Were Dettol and Band-Aid on my knee
Perhaps a tetanus injection for my crimes
And mother's words ringing "How many times ..."

My mother said for women like me
Over thirty-five no skirts above knee
And red and green should never be seen
And white at night is just not right
But sometimes I wish that mother had said
"Don't marry that man; you're in over your head!"

'Cause, quite frankly, I don't care what the neighbours might think
And I know life's too damn precious to be chained to that sink
Just remember on Earth all families are like yours
They take the good with the bad, celebrations and wars
Just remember as my great-granny said,
"Two pounds to find it out and £200,000 to hide it instead."

Bunnings Albury

This poem is about my local hardware store. I live on the border of two states, NSW and Victoria where there is a Bunnings on both sides of the Murray River. I'm not sure why but the two stores are mirror image to each other so the shelves are set up in reverse order. I'm supposed to be a free-spirited Aquarian but nothing could be further from the truth. This chaos and disorder annoys me and whenever I'm in the Wodonga aisles, I feel confused.

I wrote this poem around 2012 after the opening of a major new high-rise building in Albury, home to the Australian Tax Office (ATO). I like my poems to have a little twist at the end, so the penny-pinchers from the ATO copped it.

I like to shop at Bunnings Albury and walk among the rows
There's everything that you could want, as everybody knows
From builder's hardware, wood, and nails—to paint and plants and screws
You're sure to find it as you shop, you really just can't lose

Men go to hide there from their wives and keep the kids at bay
They love to chat between the rows on any weekend day
The tool shop in the centre is their favourite place to be
It's covered in by walls and screens for extra security

But ladies please don't feel left out among those Bunnings aisles
No need to join eHarmony, just hang around a while
The fixings aisle in number ten is where you need to be
Just pick your mark and look perplexed: "Excuse me, can you help me?"

But my favourite place is up the back between rows fifty-five and -six
It's where they put those end of lines and bits they just can't fix
You may not need that plastic tub, that paint pot, torch, or fan
But geez it's great to get a bargain when you're a handyman

There are many things I'd like to buy: that outdoor garden setting
The water feature (with the lion's head), and simply not forgetting
That lovely kitchen up the back that makes mine look quite drab
But I avoid the cleaning aisle where they sell OMO, Ajax, and FAB

Last week I came to aisle twenty-nine to buy poison for my ceiling
I got Ratsack, Talon, and Big Cheese; the mice find it quite appealing
I'll put it all up in my roof and hope the little rascals disappear
My friend says my mouse plague is my penalty for living by Albury's weir

Customer service is always helpful and there are leaflets as a guide
And a very knowledgeable gardener where the plants are kept outside
And as I exit out the door I'm sure that there will be
The aroma of a sausage sizzle to raise money for charity

But if you're from Wodonga and you shop at Bunnings there
And you come across the border, well, you'd better be beware
For Bunnings in Wodonga is built the wrong way round
'Cause the builder had a bad day and the plans were upside down

So aisle one is twenty-four and twenty-two is three
The plants are sitting on the side of where the wood should be
I do hope that builder didn't build the tax office in our town
Or sadly all the penny-pinchers will be sitting underground

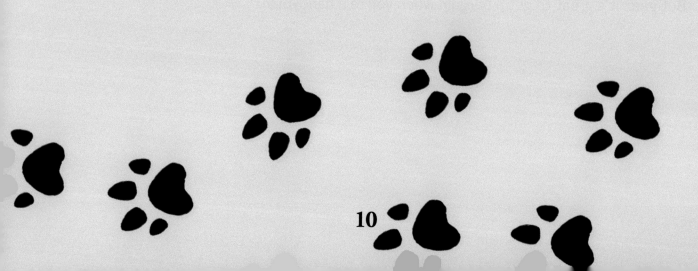

Captain Lisa Tasman Ride

F2277912   8219952

I joined the Australian Army Reserve at 3RNSWR in Canberra on 11 April 1981. I resigned in 2016 because of my Parkinson's. I was no high flyer through the ranks; I was a wife and mother first and I am very proud of my children. I have three sons: Brendan, Adon and Tasman and two daughters, Stephanie and Isobel. So, family first, and employment second: AFP, ANU, NSW Corrections, marriage celebrant, and Defence APS along the way where I often specialised in media liaison and public relations. My Army Reserve commitments had to come third. By the time I really started getting into some serious logistics and command training, Parkinson's had started to consume me. Just as the military appreciation process teaches, I had to reassess and change tactics.

My favourite years in the Army Reserve were through the 1980's and '90s as a Recruit Platoon Commander at the Regimental Training Unit, 2nd Training Group, Bardia Barracks

Ingleburn NSW. Here I was an instructor of recruits. I would finish a shift as a police officer in Canberra, hop in my Datsun Stanza and drive up to Sydney for a weekend's training. I made many friends who are still with me today. I particularly loved drill and proudly carried my grandfather Brigadier Sir Lindsay Tasman Ride's sword on many march-out parades. In 1983 RSM-A WO1 Wally Thompson complimented me at the end of my graduation parade, saying I gave the finest words of command he had ever heard a woman deliver. High praise from RSM-A.

I've never liked to say that I'm *just Army Reserve*. We all have a role to play. If I can put a pair of boots in a box in a warehouse and move them by road, rail, sea or air to a soldier on the ground overseas who requires them, then I've done my bit. I am in awe of those who serve full-time and deploy overseas to keep us safe. During OP SLIPPER (Afghanistan) I was saddened by the growing death toll of Australian soldiers, particularly the attacks on coalition forces by trusted counterparts in the Afghan National Army. These so-called "green on blue" deaths come from the colour-coding system used by the US military. Friendly NATO forces are blue personnel and the host nations are identified as green.

Sadly, the Australia media began to report that Post Traumatic Stress Disorder (PTSD) was impacting on soldiers returning from deployment. This growing toll affected me greatly. My first version of this poem was delivered at Yackandandah, Victoria on ANZAC Day 2012 by WO2 Charles Gutiez. Over time it morphed into a comment about PTSD. If your loved one's name is in my poem, I have put it there with the greatest of respect and I am sorry for your loss. RIP fine soldier. This poem is *not* a criticism of Defence who provide excellent support services both in an out of service. To any soldier (sailor or air personnel) who needs help, please *talk* to someone- and conversely, if you know someone who needs assistance, please remember the *buddy system* and seek assistance. I have included a few telephone numbers which are correct at time of printing (2016). If you need urgent assistance, dial 000.

Beyond Blue: 1300 22 4636
Soldier On: 1300 620 380
Defence Family Helpline: 1800 624 608

Oh, and if you'd like to make the best move you ever could and "do something for yourself" you could always join the Australian Army Reserve. Go to any Defence Recruiting Centre or telephone 13 19 01.

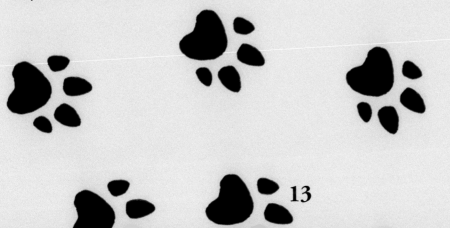

Remember the Australian Soldier

I am an Australian soldier; I stand tall and proud and true
I train and fight for freedom; I honour my country and I protect you
Established in the Sudan and Boer I've always done you proud
With volunteers and Regiments from Federation to conflicts now

The First World War (sheer tragedy) we lost too many men
And the women who supported—the nurses who cared for them
From our fateful landing upon the ANZAC Cove
The mateship that we honour is bound by all we know

To the Aussie soldier, courage, teamwork and initiative are barely but a start
For professionalism, loyalty and innovation are clearly in our heart
From World War II and wars beyond, from Vietnam to peacekeeping today
Australian soldiers are deployed around the globe from their families far away

And I know each soldier joins the ranks because they feel it too
It's the spirit of the Aussie digger; it's what we call *true blue*
But *contact front* can take a life; a new name to cast upon the wall
In bronze to forever commemorate another loss too great to call

Recently we've lost Russell, Pearce, Locke, and Wood
McCarthy, Lambert, Marks
And forty-one names for me to recite
Please keep them in your hearts

For *green on blue* is not the way a soldier's meant to die
And any loss of life through war is so hard to justify
And those returning still live the hell, the smells, sights, sounds, and fear
That follow them in dreams and thoughts, some take them to despair

14

Sadly, the number of soldiers affected by PTSD who are taking their own lives
Are far outweighed by the names cast in bronze, those men we highly prize
This growing toll also sacrificed so that we may live in peace today
Please stand tall and proud to honour that gift; God bless their souls, I pray

Give strength to those who loved them best as we remember them always
We will honour their ANZAC spirit to the very end of days
But in life's passing, their mateship is still here with you
I believe it's standing by your side
I ask that you remember the Australian soldier with love and hope and pride.

In appreciation to those who serve.

I would be honoured to have you read my poem as part of any ANZAC, Remembrance Day or other service as appropriate.

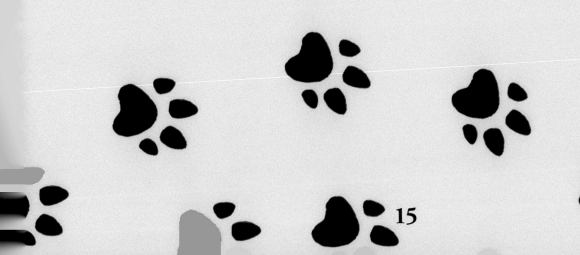

Driving to Corryong

I wrote this poem for the 2015 National Australian Bush Poetry Championships held at **The Man from Snowy River Festival** in Corryong Victoria. The poem had to mention A. B. Paterson, Jack Riley, and Corryong. I wrote the poem the day before the competition closed while seated on the train from Albury to Melbourne. The man sitting next to me did the old *I'm not reading what you're writing* trick but gave the occasional snigger. I thought to myself "I must be doing OK!" I didn't get to take a second look, edit it, or rework it in any way. When I got to Melbourne I popped it in the post box at Southern Cross Station and never gave it another thought. Well blow me down, I won *Best New Novice Writer*.

Jack Riley is the reason we all gather here today
He was the inspiration for those horses gathered at the fray
I'm sure the Irish in him was his catalyst for life
They say hot-blooded temper often got him into strife
For we know while drinking at Tom Groggin camped around the fire
That he met and kindled Banjo's thoughts and insatiable desire
To spin a yarn about those brumbies there on mountain side
And to pen a poem of glory, one of mountain men who ride

But that was then and this is now, it's not a horse you'll lose
'Cause times have changed and we all drive with everything on *cruise*
But I know the lads from Corryong are from a different breed
(It's the way they play their footy and the foods their mothers' feed)
Not many ride on horses now, they move by sterner steed
A mechanical contraption they all call the SUV
But they don't drive the way we do; the way we do down south
The way they drive is quite full-on; it leaves your heart inside your mouth

Well, I don't know if you have ever tried to drive up here at night
But it truly is a different world; it will give you quite a fright
Where I come from (down Albury way) while driving 'round the weir
The only creatures causing grief are kangaroos I fear
But let me warn you when you drive up here you'll get yourself in strife
As the creatures by the roadside have a flippant attitude to life
And just like Jack Riley's massive leap on a pony with no fear
These critters launch themselves in front of you at any time of year

And not just kangaroos, oh no, but every living thing
That runs on four legs, even two, or hoof or toe or wing
Wombats, rabbits, deer, and fox appear before your eyes
Bats, rats, even mice and owls and birds of every size
And not to mention Mother Nature and what she'll throw at you
From bushfire, flood and sleeting rain or snow drifts to drive though

So do be careful as you drive up there on Kosciusko side
Make sure you've got your wits with you and stay buckled up inside
Remember mountain creatures will be toying with your life
So take it pretty carefully or else you'll be in strife
And please don't come in *smart cars* (those environmental toys)
When driving up to Corryong you'll need to match the local boys
So strap a rifle, mount a bull-bar and put a spotty on your truck
And whack those RM Williams mudflaps on the rear to catch the muck

And the final warning that I give, the one that works for me
Is to take it slowly on the road; you **must** drive sensibly
Don't brake too hard on roads up there; there's just no room for error
Or else you'll spear down mountainside through rocks and gums in terror
'Cause there's nothing you need less in life up there on mountainside
Than to replicate behind steering wheel Jack Riley's scary ride

Clothes *do* Maketh the Exhibitor

This poem was written when I showed Dalmatians under the *Luckywood* prefix in and around Canberra, ACT in the 1990's. Showing dogs is an art form and presentation of both the dog and the exhibitor is paramount. I was horrified when a dishevelled competitor turned up in thongs and stubbies to show at the Canberra Royal when really, you should dress to impress. Dang! Where has sense and sensibility got to? Mind you, I used to exhibit in dotty skirts, dotty socks, and the like. It takes a clever handler to show the dog, not themselves.

I guess that by now you have realised that the title of my book refers to my love of Dalmatians. *Luckywood Wirlinga Belle** [2] was my favourite Dalmatian. Her pet name was 'Dottie.' Not dotty as in spots, but Dottie, short for Dorothy. She was my Dottie spotty!

Dottie was born in 2000 and was my constant companion for the next eleven years. One fateful summer evening in 2011 I took her with me to the bottom paddock of my two acres by Albury's Lake Hume Weir where I had to prime the house pump. Tragically, she was bitten by a 2m brown snake. My vet desperately tried to save her, but she passed away 24hrs later.

You know how you have that one pet that you remember above all others? The special one? Your *Greyfriar's Bobby*; the *Red Dog* in your life? Well, she was mine. Dottie is with me in my heart and is now helping me to tell my story through poetry. Let's continue on!

---

2 *Luckywood* was my registered kennel name with the Royal NSW Kennel Control.

Wirlinga Belle is the registered botanical name of a Camelia variety developed and grown on my property by the previous owner, noted horticulturalist, Mr Tom Savage

You shouldn't exhibit in thongs and stubbies
It really is quite crass
You need to show your prize new puppies
With flair and dash and class

Your dog is groomed and sprayed and powdered
Some taking many hours
So please, exhibitor take my tip
And go and have a shower

You don't need to exhibit in a tux
Or wear your best suit every time
But I'm sure that you can make an effort
To help your dog look fine

The dog is the target for the judge's eye
Conformation, condition and breeding
But a well-dressed handler surely must
Make the whole picture most appealing

So exhibiter, next time when you wake
Upon a weekend morn
Ensure you make an effort please
Or else you'll catch my scorn

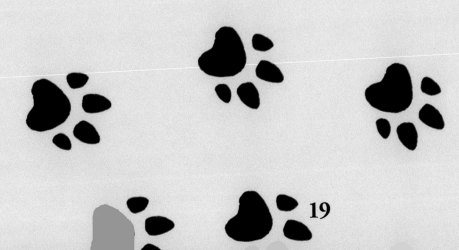

The Aldi Centre Aisle

What is the Aldi centre aisle? It's like shopping, only more competitive!

I have a small confession called the Aldi centre aisle
I know I shouldn't go there or even pause a while
Because I come out with lots of stuff I simply just don't need
But I buy it 'cause it's useful—not because of greed

When I go in I try to shop just around the sides
But it really is quite futile, for the Aldi centre aisle
Is calling me to come and see what *specials* on today
You never know what you might find inside those Aldi bays

Some shoppers get up bright and early before the crack of dawn
They're waiting for doors to open on Wednesday or Saturday morn
There're the ones you've got to watch; they know what's going on
For they've scoped the Aldi catalogue and made shopping lists quite long

Well, I've bought silicon bakeware and I don't even cook
And a *Wonder Woman* DVD collection; the acting was truly crook
And an adjustable impact hammer drill for $19.99
Although I'm not a handyman, I'm sure it will be fine

Last Saturday I bought a motorcycle jacket and a pair of pants
Today I got a ballet outfit and I can't even dance
But shopping there is lots of fun; it really is quite fine
Where else can you buy Pfeffernusse when it's Christmas time?

By the time you're at the checkout, I'm sure that you will find
That your shopping bags are fuller than what you had in mind
Don't stress or worry; when you get home pop those impulse buys away
I'm sure you'll get to use them ... one rainy winter's day!

The Call of the Currawong

This is one of my few serious poems; one that doesn't have that little kick at the end. This is a reflective poem about my reaction each year to the end of summer. The currawong's first call is a stark reminder that the long, warm, and productive days of summer are coming to a close.

It's been a long, hot summer, but the birds are on the wing
You can hear them clearly calling through the gum trees as they sing
But you'll know when summer's waning; it's a sign that's never wrong
It's the clear and steady warble of the bush bird currawong

As summer ends the golden sun sets lower in the skies
But the first time that you hear their call it's always a surprise
For the Brindabella winter will be long and cold and hard
And the cattle from the high country will be brought down to the yard

For in the heat the currawong will harbour safely in the trees
To raise their young on mountainside and savour mountain breeze
Although late in March there may be a final few days of heat to bear
By April days grow shorter and there's a crispness in the air

The currawong's swift flying movement overhead on high
Heralds wintertime approaching as they dart down from the sky
His yellow eye and wings tipped white and most distinctive call
Accompany a myriad of coloured leaves; a stunning autumn to befall

Although the currawong's appearance sometimes leaves me feeling sad
It feels like the death of summer but it's really not that bad
For the seasons follow one by one; autumn, winter, through to spring
As with the currawong's appearance, I just wouldn't change a thing

It's Only Disqualified Driving

This poem is about those on our roads who drive unlicensed. Who knows how many there are? I've made a guess in my poem and suggest it's perhaps one in ten. It never ceases to amaze me how difficult (and expensive) it is to obtain a licence. Perhaps there's the answer to the question. Maybe it's easier *not* to obtain one but with increasing technology it's getting difficult to remain undetected.

I've always maintained it's a privilege not a right to hold a licence. The reference to "the right to silence" and the "one phone call" come from American TV shows. In Australia there's no such thing. This poem comes to you from my experiences as a police officer in the AFP and from my work in NSW Corrections, both in the Court House and case managing offenders.

I'm driving down the road one day as I am wont to do
When suddenly in my rear-view mirror I spied a nasty view
The traffic car from Albury LAC[3] was right there on my tail
And as I indicated left I turned a whiter shade of pale

I don't know why I did it but something just clicked inside
This cop knows I'm not registered; I'll take him for a ride
There pulled up on the street I watched him exit out his door
And as he walked up to my car, I put my foot flat to the floor

Through a cloud of dust in Mate Street all I could plainly see
Was the copper sprinting to his car; now he's pursuing me
My VL Commodore's running hot and I haven't got that far
When I slide her through the five-ways, narrowly missing several cars

But once again the vision in my rear view isn't very kind
There's lights all flashing red and blue; 203's[4] on my behind
Screeching left into Urana Road I nearly didn't make the turn
My slick tyres now are smoking hot and my engine starts to burn

---

3 Local area command.
4 Traffic car call-sign.

And the dash lit up with warning lights; it's not looking good for me
'Cause the last time that I had this car serviced was back in 1993
So I put my foot flat to the floor to give her one last go
But with one almighty bang that was that..... and the engine there did blow

And just near Coles in Lavington my car she went no more
Next thing I know I'm pulled out of the car and cuffed beside the door
No, of course I don't have a licence; you spoke to me last week
After I stole that Nissan Bluebird and dumped it in the creek.

Just near Mungabareena, my place of choice to burn the cars
That I've previously stolen late at night parked outside Albury bars
Like *Paddy's* or the *Bended* or even at *The Star*
Where punters go to have a drink and forget to lock their car

This stupid number plate recognition system is giving up the game
I just can't drive unregistered no more; it really is quite lame
As you know, I've never held a licence, either probationary or full
For I never passed the computer test while a *Learner* still at school.

For "*it's only disqualified driving*" I've been done nine times before
And found myself in a truth suit on Mr. Murray's Albury courtroom floor
I've done the Bonds, Community Service; I'm a very special client
Of Community Offender Services (although I've never been compliant)

And don't touch me now you stupid cop 'cause I know all my rights
You'd better watch your back when you walk out the station late at night
I'm going to take my right to silence and demand that one phone call
From the payphone that is hanging in the lock-up on the wall

And my brief from Legal Aid will have me right back on the street
After court sits in the morning and I assure you I'll repeat
The offences that I committed today; I'll be driving there next to you
They say one in ten drivers is unlicensed–bloody scary, but it's true!

Cougars at the Kinross

The Kinross is a former sheep station converted into a restaurant, bar, and concert venue. It's predominately country music and boot scooting. The girls and I went there New Year's Eve 2015. In writing this poem I have changed names to protect the innocent! We aren't really cougars, but the title was irresistible. Just remember, ladies, as I say: "Never wear leopard print after the age of fifty- or you'll look like a cougar".

It's New Year's Eve, and there I am in pyjamas home alone
When suddenly there's a beeping noise–a text message on my phone.
The girls are in their glad rags; they've all applied their lippy gloss
And decided that the place to party is in Thurgoona at Kinross.

My friend Rachel is really hassling me and says I must come too,
And although I try to say I can't, there's just no time to think it through.
The next SMS is frightening because she's right outside my door.
I'd better get dressed super-fast and pick my jaw up off the floor.

Luckily I had my hair done a little earlier in the day.
I throw on a dress, grab my bag and phone, and we'll soon be on our way.
The dog and cat give me puzzled looks as I'm whisked away from home.
Party time? NYE? Past my bedtime? I'm right outside my zone!

I have not stayed up past midnight, gosh, I think since Y2K,
When we feared computer failure and the bug stealing funds away.
Now I wonder if I am even capable of staying awake and upright after ten
Let alone dancing, drinking, or miraculously attracting single men.

I don't know all of Rachel's friends with me inside the car,
So she introduces me to them and tells them I'm a star.
Explains that I'm a poet and mentions trophies I have won,
So I entertain them endlessly as we drive up Highway 31.

Rachel's such a party planner; she's reserved a table in her name.
Lucky that she did that or things just wouldn't be the same.
We would have had a table up the hallway near the loo,
Or worse out on the paddock deck with aroma of sheep poo.

Now, the chefs are great at Kinross, and I had a very tasty meal.
A *Chicken Little* kid-sized nugget plate a friend ordered to conceal
My actual age and size (now steady on no need to be so rude).
Why don't they let you buy small portions? It's still just selling food!

And I recited all through dinnertime to keep my friends well entertained,
And they laughed at all my poetry while little kids fell off the stage.
Later the crowd was pretty light; I said there'd be no hope for us,
But luckily a group of local farmers arrived at the Kinross on a bus.

But men our age only have eyes for girls with short skirts way up high.
I call them Pussy Pelmets; strips of fabric for the thigh
As if they're going to look at me; I'm halfway to The Grange.
I'm sure most of them drive sports cars and chase women half my age

And later Mary-Ann turned up to join us with her ex beside her too.
(But I can tell by body language that relationship ain't through.)
She told me his name is John; he drives a truck so couldn't drink.
If he gets breath tested in the morning, he could end up inside the clink.

And after dinner we found a spot on bar stools in a good position near the door.
We had a clear view of everything, even the girl who collapsed upon the floor.
She left the Kinross by ambulance; gosh you'd think it would've been me,
But blow me down I was still all possum-eyed at twenty-two past three.

What a great night I had with Rachel, Sarah, Fiona, Pat, and Gwendolyn.
Together this tough party of women celebrated seeing 2016 in.
We partied hard to that band from Goulburn; three guys with great music covers,
But sadly since that night I've discovered it takes more than three days to recover.

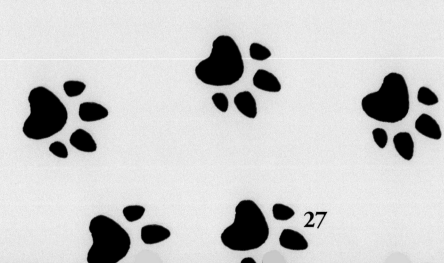

Sterling Stephanie

My eldest daughter's name is Stephanie but this poem is not about her. I'm a quilter and I collect vintage sewing machines. I'm a member of an online sewing group where one of our members in America came across something unusual in a Singer sewing machine treadle drawer that she had purchased. It contained a rare Singer Sterling .22 pistol.

The Singer 222K is a small portable sewing machine that every quilter lusts after.

Steph bought herself a cabinet to stow her Singer sewing machine
But when she went to clean it out she found the strangest thing she'd seen
Expecting thimbles, needles, thread, some pins or patterns too
She got a rather strange surprise for she found a twenty-two

She put a comment there online (as she has done before)
About the contents she had scored when cleaning out that drawer
But the ladies on the Facebook site were clearly all a flutter
Their comments posted thick and fast; some pursed their lips and tutted

"Silly Steph! The Singer most highly prized is a Singer 222"
"No, you don't understand," she cried. "It's a Singer twenty-two!"
For there, right in that small top drawer was a Sterling Singer .22 pistol
Usually its fluff and pins I find, I always get a fistful

Now, some would say that's overkill … excuse my little pun
But Stephanie's clearly packing 'cause she found that Singer gun
So may I suggest you don't take her sewing scissors to cut paper in any way
Or else you could hear these fateful words from her:
"Go right ahead and *make my day*!"

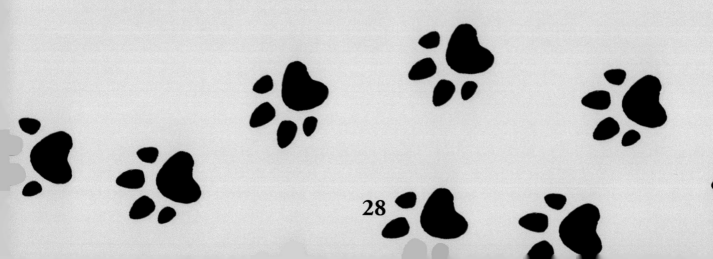

The Fabric Stash

I wrote this poem around 2000. It was published in *Homespun* magazine under my former married name of Lisa Bailey. It also won me an eBook in 2014 when I posted it in the Martingale *Stitch This!* Blog because it had the most number of "likes" across the US that week. On my travels I've seen this poem framed and on the wall of a patchwork shop in both Townsville and Perth.

For those of you who are not quilters, fat eighths and fat quarters are fabric lengths cut from a bolt or roll of patchwork fabric. Quilt groups and guilds, feel free to share my poem.

I have a little problem
It's called my fabric stash
My husband doesn't know it
But it cost a lot of cash
It started out as remnant pieces
I bought from a shop
But it then became addictive,
And I really couldn't stop

Fat eighths became fat quarters
Two metres became three
But when I purchased a whole bolt
I sought psychiatry.
I just can't pass your patchwork shop
I have to come and see
If there is any missing piece
Inside that might suit me

So hubby starts to realise
One fabric cupboard becomes two
He keeps me from your patchwork shop
To keep our marriage true
So I sit at my computer
While I'm banished to the house
But he'll have to hide the Visa card
'cause I still can click a mouse

Well, there isn't any answer
To this tale of fabric woe
For this hobby is delightful
And your fabric stash will grow[5]
Just remember the old saying
As you purchase with a grin
"She who dies with the most fabric … wins!"

---

5 An earlier version had:
For children grow and leave you
And husbands come and go
but when reciting to older ladies some used to look at me disapprovingly, so I changed it!

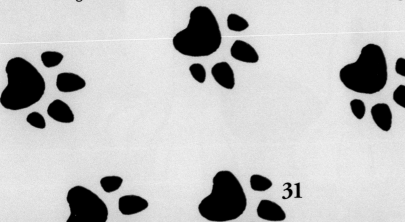

The Seven Deadly Sins

For a short time I belonged to a local writing group at the Albury Library Museum. At the end of class each week we were given a topic for homework. I must confess that when the seven deadly sins were assigned to me, I had to go home and look them up. In my research, not only did I find seven sins, I discovered seven antidotes. This poem is long in length and quite deep in meaning. Scattered throughout you will find many references to church, piety and finding your way to heaven. Bizarrely, this poem just flowed onto the page!

There are seven deadly sins you know; I Googled them online
And there they were in black and white so now I'll take the time
To share with you the secrets of this very important list
I'll check them one by one with you, lest you're a hedonist

The first is *lust* considered by some as the deadliest sin of man
To say the word out loud makes me blush; oh please pass me a fan
Intense desire, not only for sex; it could be money, power or fame
Put Dante's *Purgatorio*'s unforgiven souls into a fiery pit of flame
But thankfully the antidote to lust is *chastity* for sure
Though I don't know where the key to my belt went ...
Maybe it fell through a crack in the floor?

The second *gluttony* is not so bad, or so it seems to me
My love of chocolate quickly consumed ever so greedily
But overconsumption to the point of waste is what they're trying to teach
Hopefully to share your lot around and not keep others out of reach
For gluttony is selfish and this tendency to sin
Will see your selfishness unrewarded for not letting others in
The antidote is *temperance*; I can hear your feeble moans.
But the only Temperance I can recall is the scientist in *Bones*

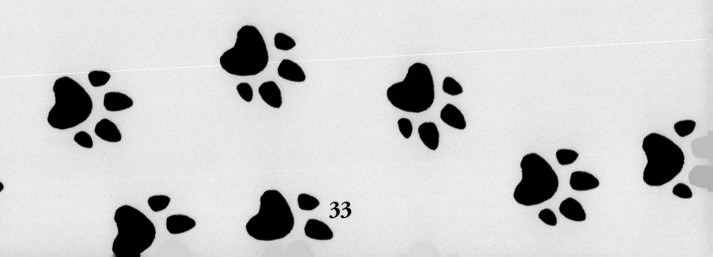

The third is *greed* also known as avarice (now I had to look that up)
It's the sin of excess, cupidity or covetousness, to overflow your cup
So don't amass great piles of things and be careful of possession
Or you'll possibly compromise any chance you have of getting into heaven
So someone kindly put a lock onto my password, my entry to eBay
And cut up all my credit cards and throw my cheques away
For here my cure is *charity*; I've heard of her before
I'll endeavour to keep my ear out when she's knocking at my door

Number four is *sloth* which can be interpreted two ways
Defined as physical or spiritual laziness to the very end of days
But I always visualise sloth as a lazy creature up in a tree
Which I can assure you now is not at all like me
For I attack the things I do at a very rapid rate
Perhaps it's time for *diligence* to help me compensate
This sin perhaps throughout my life has most affected me
But just in action, not in words, and never spiritually

Five is *wrath* a nasty one of hatred, anger and rage
The sin that hurts us all with spite at any tender age
For someone who is hard of heart is just no fun at all
Their cutting words of revenge, jealousy and anger will befall
Patience here will rescue them with her capacity for calm endurance
Tolerance and understanding wipes self-destructiveness; I give you my assurance

Envy comes at number six characterised by insatiable desire
She's the one you've got to watch; she leaves your heart on fire
For envy only poisons you and makes you sorrow for another's good
You're not supposed to wish your house looked like another in your 'hood
Kindness will relieve you here and make you see for sure
In confession acceptance is the way to go; it'll see you through the door

And here we are at number seven *pride* the final sin of all
The one the old saying always tells you comes before a fall.
It's the most deadly sin of all and the one that consumes us all the most
And keeps us further from the Trinity: Father, Son and Holy Ghost
Humility's your virtue here to save you from the fire
To cast out all your selfish thoughts, to this you must aspire

So now you know the yin and yang; I've explained to you the list
I hope you listened carefully and there's nothing that you missed
'Cause you only get one go at it when living out your life
And walking in the sinner's shoes will surely get you into strife
So choose your path with carefulness and come along with me
But could you let me know when someone finds my little key?

Christmas

I do love Christmas but to me it just gets harder every year. Perhaps as you get older the gloss of Christmas gets mixed in with unreal expectations, family drama and the cost. The commercialisation of Christmas means we've lost our way in its true meaning. The last grocery shop before Christmas Day is quite frankly, hell and God forbid if Nanna should have to find a different car park from the one she's parked in for the last sixty-five years!

Christmas ... the very sound of the word, it fills my heart with fear
Although it comes around the same day December twenty-fifth every year
You'd think the sky is falling or that the world had come to an end
It's the time of year when grocery shopping can send you completely 'round the bend

For although the shops are going to shut for only but a day
The scrum for loaves of bread and milk puts football games to shame
I've seen one lady get knocked out, another lose an eye
As she made that horror, fateful leap to reach the last mince pie

And Christmas just gets earlier; it's coming round way too soon
Surely it must be illegal to erect Christmas trees in June?
For Christmas is the day we should celebrate our dear Christ Jesus' birth
Not some middle-aged bearded man's commercialised expanding girth

And I've never really understood why Christmas visions show
Reindeer standing ankle deep in drifts of pure white snow
For Christmas here from where I stand is forty-three degrees
And the only frosting I will see will be in my deep freeze

And mums and dads with screaming kids please stay at home I pray
To buy Christmas vouchers while online and your presents on eBay
But hurry!
Let's clear those shelves at Boxing Day sales to make room for the new display
Of Easter eggs and hot cross buns just in time for ....Australia Day!

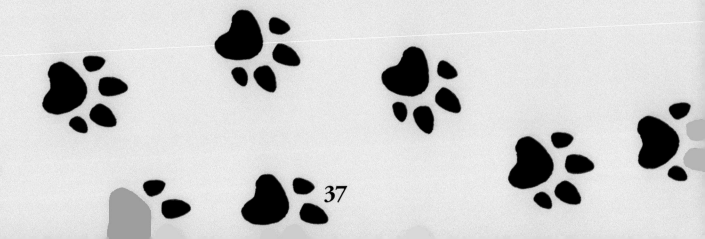

The Op-Shopping Towney

I do love op-shopping (thrift stores) and still recycle all my clothes. As these volunteer run shops become businesses', it is getting harder to find true bargains but as they say "one man's trash is another man's treasure" and I still get enough wins to keep going back.

My definition of a towney is a city dweller who goes out to the country in full outback gear: an Akubra hat, Ariat boots and RM Williams jeans complete with oversized cowboy belt buckle. Invariably the clothes are brand new with not a speck of dust on them. The towney drives a sport utility vehicle, or SUV with absolutely no off-road capability. I call these vehicles 'grocery gatherers.' In this poem I refer to my SUV as a *faux-wheel drive*, a play on words. I'm pretty sure my car has the off-road capability of a ballerina in a tutu.

Sadly after my arrival in Albury in 1998 for a couple of years I was undoubtedly the best dressed towney around!

I've got a little issue with my wardrobe—it's too small
It's packed right to the gunnels; there's no room in it at all
But I'm grateful it's a walk-in, 'cause I'll roll in a stand
But now that's chockers also; lucky I don't have a man

I think clothes are my obsession and I just can't get enough
But I op-shop and I justify and say it's all *preloved*
'Cause you're the silly person that pays for it full price
But I buy my clothes at Vinnies and I think they're just as nice

But instead of paying half my wages, I just pay five bucks
But op-shopping is a lotto and you have to have good luck
Some days you're empty-handed, some days you have a win
They're the days you come out smiling with a Cheshire grin

But I've also got a hankering for anything RM
I wear their gear from head to foot which always gets a grin
From graziers who pass into town; they find it quite a hoot
That I've got golden horns emblazoned on my RAV4 boot

I've got enough RM stuff to kit out a whole yard
Of farmers and producers; it really wouldn't be that hard
But when a new catalogue comes out I'll be waiting by the door
Of my local RM clothing shop because I've just got to have some more

But if I'm in an op-shop and I find my holy grail
Some RM on a hanger well, I'll never ever fail
To pay the money, give a cheer and run right out that door
It's almost better than the DFO[6] and cheaper too, for sure

But if you're in the country and you see me driving in
Don't worry that I'll go *off-road* or cause you any din
For I've only got the **faux** wheel drive; the RAV4, she's a two
This towney's on an op-shop mission and she's only passing through

---

6 Direct Factory Outlet

39

The Hot Favourite

I was asked to entertain at the Aspire Marquee at Albury Race Course for Oaks Day 2015. This day is for the ladies and the Fashions on the Field competition is hotly contested. It's a day of couture dresses, millinery and coordinated accessories. Lizzie Pogson runs this event each year. In 2014 I stood up and volunteered to read a poem. In 2015 I was asked to write one specifically for the day, so I wrote *The Hot Favourite* and the ladies loved it. I had help from my dear friend Tracy Caines who assisted me with race terminology.

In addition I wrote a very naughty poem called *LBL can go to Hell* to help sell an intimate lady's procedure. It brought the house down! I thought long and hard about putting it in this book but it failed the 'mother test'!

Oaks Day at Albury Race Course puts the fillies right on show
It's the time to kick your heels up; you know you really ought to go
And see the lovely ladies leaning on the racecourse fence
The theme this year is floral with a touch of elegance

And near the betting circle you will find Aspire Marquee
Where generous souls will once again raise funds for charity
Your MC will be Narelle today, she's good at real estate
But instead of selling homes she's calling at the starter's gate

Now as women you know there's work to do before you can lean upon that fence
It's not just dress, bag, hat and shoes; let's call it *maintenance*
But unfortunately for me this is where I come undone
'Cause there's weeks and weeks of tweaking before I'll see the those races run

I'm way too old to be a filly, for me no fashions on the field
I've even gone past brood mare so they scratched me; my fate's sealed
It all started at the hairdresser where I went to have a '*do*'[7]
She said blandly "This won't take too much time!" as she pulled a small comb through

---

7 Hair-do

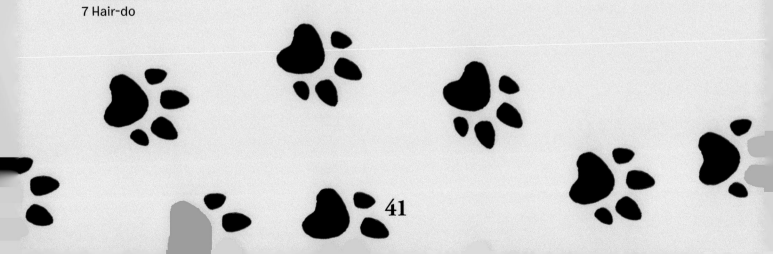

You see I sport a sad comb-over; I've never had lush hair
So in order to disguise it I'll plonk a fascinator there
And with bleaching, waxing, shaving I should be rid of other hair
I wish it would grow as luscious above as it flourishes *down there*

So by the time I've done my makeup, found my hat and shoes and bag
Tried on sixteen hundred dresses, I still look like some tired old silly nag
And don't you just hate it when that pert young thing at Myer
Sashays past the mirror saying:
"It's the first dress that I've tried on. It's just perfect! I'm on fire!"

But I think I finally got it right, I hope I'm not mutton dressed as lamb
I've bought clever undergarments to hold it all tight and disguise anything I can
And please don't mention stupid spray-on tans
It's frankly getting all too hard
I'd rather concentrate on drinking now and holding up that bar

Which brings me to another point; I hope you don't intend to drive
You should have organised a lift by now to arrive home safe alive
And one final word of caution that I must pass on to you
Is in regards to alcohol and every word is true

Because after you've had several drinks that unappealing man in crappy suit
Starts to look like he's Adonis, although he's clearly got no loot
You'll end up stumbling through the car park, shoes a-swingin' in your hand
The cougar's long walk of shame to Fallon Street may not be something that you planned

So enjoy yourself with girlfriends- I know Albury Race Course catering is grand
And I hope you'll donate generously with that money in your hand
As Lizzie and her team of helpers raise funds so tirelessly
Hopefully you're odds-on favourite, not a one hundred to one shot, like me

In Praise of Podiatry

Did you know there's a difference between the podiatric and orthopaedic Medicare rebate in Australia? I didn't until I chose a podiatric surgeon. I was in terrible agony from a heel spur. Luckily Dr Kingsford squeezed me into his busy surgery list when there was a sudden cancellation. I vaguely remember him informing me about the different rebates but all I wanted was to be out of pain, and besides, I chose my surgeon for his wonderful reputation.

After surgery I attended the doctor's consulting rooms to have dressings changed on my foot. He's a big fan of bush poetry and he listened patiently while I recited some of my work. He gave me that first inkling of encouragement to publish. One time between consultations I spied him at The Commercial Club restaurant where I go to have my favourite meal, the *Beef & Reef.*

I'm referred to Dr. Kingsford; he's going to fix my feet
'Cause I've got awful bunions and a hammertoe complete
But just as I turned fifty, I swore I'd never be
That middle-aged lady wearing runners down the street

I'd bought pairs of those orthotic shoes with the special insert for your heel
But until designers got them right, their shoes had limited appeal
Except my dog who loved them and consumed them with delight
Buying replacements monthly gave my Visa card a fright

Kumfs, Clouds and Ziera, they've all been on my feet
My penance for years of army drill and policing on the beat
But when you're young you never think of corns in years to come
Because you're ten-foot tall and bulletproof and don't think of damage done

So Dr Kingsford says I should have an x-ray just to see
The extent of damage that I have done by living fearlessly
And there, just to top it off, I even heard him say
"That's the most magnificent heel spur I've seen until this day!"

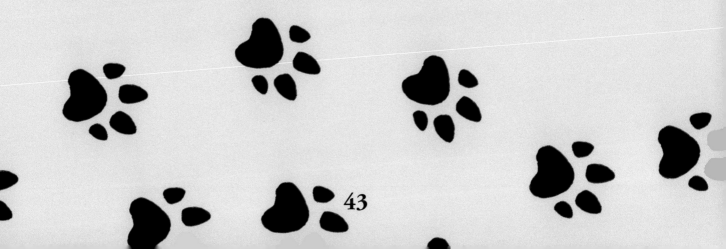

44

44

Luckily he travels from Melbourne to our Albury Wodonga town
To keep our feet nice and straight and our bunions all ground down
But I know why he really does it, because he likes to eat the dinner
The Commercial Club's Golf Club chef, he truly is a winner

So now I lie in surgery and I really am quite scared
Because the doctor and anaesthetist are grooving round my bed
They didn't think I'd hear them, they thought I was asleep
But Gregorian chant was blaring along with those monitors that beep

I'm sure the surgeon's done a lovely job of deconstructing all my crimes
And I just can't wait to wear some real shoes more suited to the times
'Cause there's nothing worse than going to a party in a dress
With runners on your feet that simply fail to impress

And young ladies just remember as you teeter on those heels
Of this warning that I give to you to prevent your later squeals
Not necessarily from the surgery or the pain that you may rue
But the lack of podiatric rebate from that stingy Medicare crew

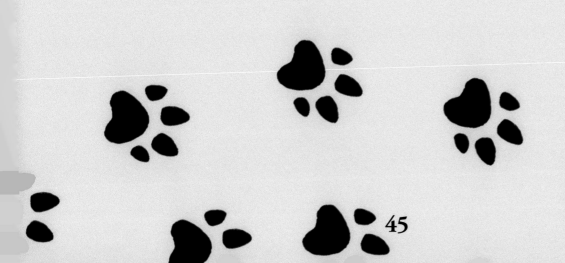

EBay and Elephants

Buying online can be hazardous, especially at four in the morning. Did I really click *Buy it now*?

I started up a small account to try to sell online
But listing all my items took up loads of precious time
And as I researched everything to see what I could get
I found lots of other things to buy but I've still got no regret

See it doesn't matter if you call it eBay, Craigslist or Gumtree
The idea is to sell your wares not buy more, apparently
But when I tried car-boot, garage, auction and clearing sale
I came home with other seller's junk and my family all yelled "Fail!"

You see I'm a *Turbo Seller* I've got two thousand stars
I didn't just get that reputation you know by hanging round in bars
But unfortunately that's not the record number listed for my sales
Because I'm a five star purchaser, the best, the Holy Grail

I never thought that I'd be caught, I thought that I had got away
With concealing all my crime of purchasing while surfing on eBay
But there it is in black and white, it's on the feedback screen
That I'm undoubtedly the best purchaser that they have ever seen

Five stars, *Super Buyer* and *Welcome back any time!*
With glowing words like this it's awfully hard to hide my crime
And don't tell me not to look online; it's futile can't you see?
'Cause sniping other buyers is a most joyous place to be

I try so very hard to sleep at night and not look at my phone
But when I wake at 4:00 a.m. it's rather lonely on your own
And right by my bed there on the app to surf at my delight
Is my *favourites* feed to entertain me in the darkness of the night

But it's not at all like gambling (a sobering lesson that some must learn)
For on eBay before you purchase there's a button marked *confirm*
But I've found it's not so easy when you wake later in the day
To explain to family members why you bought that elephant on eBay

So I've got cupboards packed with boxes of the specials that I buy
For every single purchase I will always justify
Not only are my cupboards full and underneath the bed
The garage is plainly bulging..... I'll think I'll go online and buy a shed!

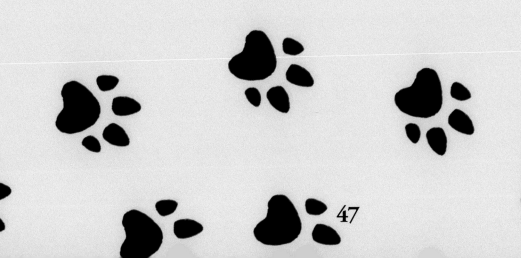

Domestic Bliss

I do apologise, gentle reader; please avert your eyes now if you have a sensitive mind.

I put it in a safe place, I know I put it there
When I went to find it, it had vanished in thin air
It's like I'm in the *Twilight Zone*; I can't seem to get things right
And it really doesn't help me that I toss and turn all night

At home I walk from room to room then wonder why I'm there
Have I just been up or down when I stand on my top stair?
Even making lists you'd think would make my life a little more exciting
But it doesn't help me, not one bit as even I can't read my writing

As I carefully put things away, I'm thinking to myself
Surely it will be safer in that drawer than there upon the shelf?
But when it's time to find the item that I have stashed away
It's like gremlins snuck in overnight and stole my things away

My mind says: *"You put it there. I know you did—there inside that drawer!"*
But the evidence is pretty clear because it's not there anymore
And it's not domestic blindness; the ailment all men all suffer from
Where you explain *exactly* where to find it but they say: "It's not there it's gone!"

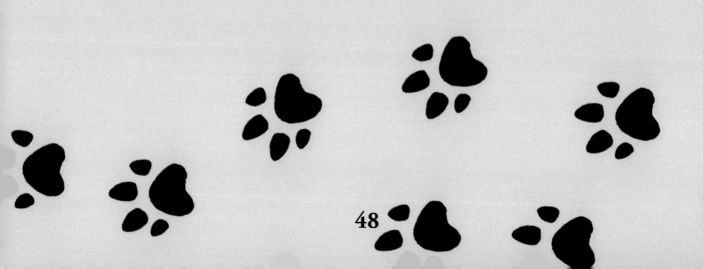

Even giving men precise location of exactly where it lies
No man will ever find it, although it's right before his eyes
Eventually you'll give up asking and show him that it's there
It most surely will be, it never fails; it sends women to despair

This ailment goes hand in hand with domestic deafness...it's true
Although the level depends on the volume your man sets his hearing capacity to
With chores like bin night, washing up, or going outside to mow
I can assure you 100% he'll have his hearing reception set down to *low*

But quietly ask the question in whispered tones; "Honey, would you like a beer?
Don't worry about helping me tonight; why don't you disappear
Down into your man-cave? There's no need to help me out!"
I can assure now one hundred per cent, there will be no need to shout

It's like when you first get married, you're the happy bride and groom
You love each other dearly and have sex in every room
A little later on there's bills and kids, pressure, doom and gloom
Lucky if you get two minutes once a week behind the locked door of your room

And I do hope you don't descend to the horror of only having hallway sex
Where you hate each other with a passion; now you're calling him your ex
Cause hallway sex isn't very nice as your relationship is through
You sleep in separate rooms, pass in the hallway, glare, and say, "F*ck YOU!"

Barramundi Bling

I wrote this poem for my friend's marriage of 30th April 2016. As you will see I wrote it to read out as the MC for their wedding reception. When I recited the poem to the bride and groom for the first time, there was a stunned silence. I was horrified. I thought I'd missed the mark but after the awkward silence, Sandy looked me in the eyes and said, "How did you do that? Everything's in there ... it's perfect." Phew! Even though *I can't get no satisfaction*, I wish them all the very best. Do read on!

Hello! My name is Lisa and I'll be your MC
But they really shouldn't have asked me 'cause I simply just don't see
The reason for any marriage as I'm feeling no attraction
For sadly I've been married three times and *I just can't get no satisfaction!*

But they say marriage is true love; a commitment for life
And today Sandy took Wendy and made her his wife
And we all stood out with them before celebrant Ian
You've travelled from all parts down here just to see 'em

So how did they meet and what started their story?
I'll not mince my words; I like to embellish with glory
But I'm secretly jealous, oh, I wish I could be
As plainly besotted as this couple, you see

So I'll tell you a tale, now let's see how it ends
It's a story of two people who started out friends
For Sandy and Wendy have long been my mates
Over Moscato and a chat by *Be-Quilted's* [8]back gate

---

8 A Long-arm quilting business

For Wendy's a patchworker and her stitches are fine
She toils on her long-arm with quilting designs
But it's rumoured the patterns for the quilts on your bed
Are designs made by Sandy in Wilson Transformer's back shed

And Sandy's got breeding that is simply a hoot
Dad's Ukrainian, Mum's Italian; born in Scotland, to boot
So don't ever cross him in the darkness of night
But he's good with his money, and he's never been tight

But clearly "mature," they've both lived life to the full
In Wendy's kitchen years later, they sure felt the pull
Of heart strings while standing there both broken-hearted
As they pondered life's journeys and relationships parted

Suddenly, obtaining some ice, Wendy felt quite surprised
For her heart skipped a beat as she looked into his eyes
And two soul mates knew instantly (although broken-hearted)
And they fell in love there with freezer door parted

Her reaction the next day, she questioned with me
"He's the sexiest bugger that I've ever seen!"
But I hoped that I calmed and I quelled all her fear
"I'm sure they won't think you're a cougar, my dear!"

Over time love blossomed while fishing out there on the weir
But Wendy's much better at fishing than Sandy, I fear
For she always hooks bigger ones out of the water
You'd expect nothing less from the fishery inspector's daughter

And they fished from the Quintrex, a tinny of note
But it quickly transpired that they'd need a new boat
For the tinny was struggling there under the weight
So the *Savage Queen Mary* was the chosen upgrade

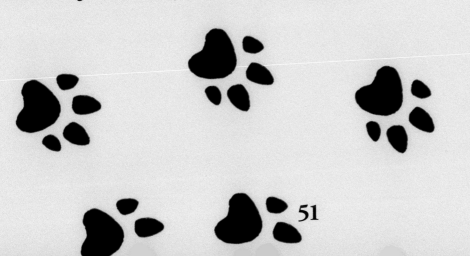

The new boat's much larger and she's ready to go
With provisions in eskys stored safe down below
Each weekend Sandy camps and fishes with Wendy his mate
You can tell they're away by the piss-ant sized lock on their gate

So continuing on they have built a love shack
Up there at Khancoban, where they both have the knack
Of enjoying good company and having a drink–
Sandy's mug of grappa, Wendy's wine glass the size of a sink

Now Sandy informs me that she buys by the cask
But buying her alcohol's no easy task
For she drives down to Rutherglen to purchase her goon[9]
She's buying so much it could drown a platoon

But she won't waste any wine; she will catch it with flair
Underneath her cask spout by the back kitchen stair
There's a small port glass awaiting to catch any stray drip
That should mystically fall from the top of its tip

Well, there's a moment of rashness in every man's life
When he thinks he's in love and is needing a wife
So Sandy planned carefully and bought himself bling
In the shape of a diamond on top of a ring.

He hatched and he schemed and planned an idea
To travel to Darwin and fish from a pier.
There, hook a big fish with a ring in its mouth
And propose to his Wendy, his girl from down south

_____

9 alcohol

Now, poor Sandy as nervous as one man can get
With diamond in pocket, now choked with regret
Gave a roll of his eyes as Wendy challenged the guard
At airport security where concealment was hard

Now Wendy's had surgery down there on her knee
And the scanner lit up like a bright Christmas tree
But the problem I speak of, that I now relate
Was the treatment of Wendy by the guard at the gate

As Wendy gave the guard *the look* Sandy gave a yelp.
Wendy was told to assume the position beside that security belt
A thorough pat-down search, swipey tests for drugs *and* bomb residue
Gave Sandy quite sufficient time to slip that diamond through

And holidaying up near Darwin, Sandy pulled it off, it's true
For on that fishing expedition he had worded up the crew
There as Wendy hooked that barramundi with a ring inside its mouth
He got down on bended knee proposing to his feisty Sheila from down south

Now, I've been told there wasn't a dry eye on the fishing boat that day
Even the burley captain got a lump in his throat and blinked some tears away
Luckily this bride and groom are older than most, you'll see
(The benefit is that they'll likely bypass the Child Support Agency)

So my story is completed now and I'm sure that it's a winner
As MC I say please sit back, relax and partake of wedding dinner
Sandy and Wendy, ensure you live your lives to the full, enjoying everything
And may your love be ever captured in the glint of barramundi bling

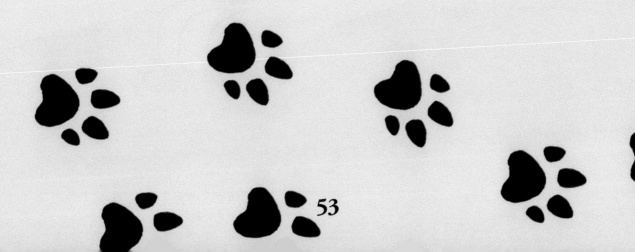

Spotty Spelling

Here's one for the kids!

How do you spell *Dalmatian*?
It's a real consternation
I see it spelt wrong all the time
So let me show you now in rhyme
Because it fills my heart with woe
When I see Dalmatian spelt with **O**

Once you learn this trick from me
You'll spell Dalmatian easily
Dalmatian starts with the letter **D**
Then follow letters **A** and **L, M, A** and **T**
And to finish spelling at the end
Just add an **I** an **A** and then an **N**

The spotty dog is only spelt with an **A**
There's three of them in quick array.
Never spell Dalmatian with an **O**
Or it's off to spelling class you'll go
Please spell Dalmatian with just the letter **A**
And then you'll really make my day!

Shaken not Stirred

This poem is about my condition; I hate to call it a *disease*
But that's the way they label it, and you can tell that I'm displeased
See, I'm only in my fifties; the time when most folks plan their life
With cruises down the Danube ... but I find myself in strife
Because dumb old Mr Parkinson's is with me as I stride
And this vision of my retirement isn't quite what I had in mind

I'd have to say right from the start that I have never been
The most coordinated person you're likely to have seen
Any games with balls involved I'd try hard not to play
No invites to join their teams—they'd run the other way
You see, I run like a duck with legs all splayed, arms flapping all about
Games with balls, they just don't suit; as if there's any doubt
I simply just can't catch anything that you might hurl at me
I'm completely uncoordinated; it's so very plain to see

And please don't mention dancing class or anything in tights
Throughout my life I've tried so hard, I've tried with all my might
Sadly, coordination eludes me here; it's really been quite bad
For when you're in a dance class, all the dancers get so mad
'Cause they're all dancing perfectly, all dancing round and round
But no matter how I try to get it right, when they're all up ... I'm down

So never throw a ball at me as your team will have a loss
I'll never catch it in my hands; my arms flail in a cross
And if I should have to be a part of any team you're in
Please confirm with me before you go which goal post gets a win?
For the only goal I ever scored was the best I've ever done
But I scored it for the other side and for that I came undone

So team sports aren't my forte; you'd think I'd do OK alone
But now with cursed Parkinson's I'm still not in my zone
It's been some years since I was told "You have Parkinson's Disease"
But it's not a diagnosis anyone wants or accepts with any ease
I tried to hide it from *the job*; it really was quite tragic
A police officer's Glock should be a single shot, not fire on automatic

But there are some benefits to my plight; I know this to be true
While cooking in the kitchen I don't read directions through
No need for me to shake the contents to ensure that they are mixed
'Cause I've already done that just by getting out the bits

So I sit at home and watch those silly pensioner ads on my TV
Where baby boomers ride bikes in parks and bounce grandkids on their knee
But I just wobble from my chair and try to walk outside
Without freezing in a doorway or tripping in my stride

There are minor gains for me it's true, when I am medicated
I work on radio 2REM and read out ads; I'm truly dedicated
But "Parky's" meds affect me like a chipmunk high on speed
I can get five hundred words quite clearly in a thirty second feed

But Parkinson's won't beat me; I'll just find another way
To fight this battle as I go and get though every single day
Although my quilting stitches these days are large and quite absurd
Mr Parkinson's can take a flying leap because I'm shaken here, not stirred

Keep a spot on your shelf for my next book!

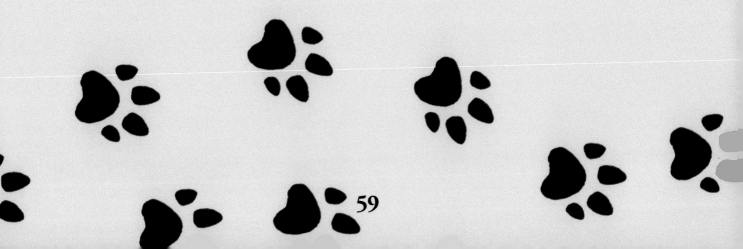

Printed in the United States
By Bookmasters